3-16

AMAZING SUPER SIMPLE INVENTIONS

SUPER SIMPLE

TELEPHONE

PROJECTS

INSPIRING & EDUCATIONAL
SCIENCE ACTIVITIES

ALEX KUSKOWSKI

Consulting Editor, Diane Craig, M.A./Reading Specialist

Super Sandcastle

An Imprint of Abdo Publishing
abdopublishing.com

abdopublishing.com

Published by Abdo Publishing, a division of ABDO, PO Box 398166, Minneapolis, Minnesota 55439. Copyright © 2016 by Abdo Consulting Group, Inc. International copyrights reserved in all countries. No part of this book may be reproduced in any form without written permission from the publisher. Super SandCastle™ is a trademark and logo of Abdo Publishing.

Printed in the United States of America, North Mankato, Minnesota
062015
092015

THIS BOOK CONTAINS
RECYCLED MATERIALS

Editor: Liz Salzmann
Content Developer: Nancy Tuminelly
Cover and Interior Design and Production: Mighty Media, Inc.
Photo Credits: Library of Congress, Mighty Media, Inc.,
Shutterstock, Wikicommons

The following manufacturers/names appearing in this book are trademarks: 3M™, Eveready®, Gedney®, Rayovac®, Slinky®

Library of Congress Cataloging-in-Publication Data

Kuskowski, Alex, author.
  Super simple telephone projects : inspiring & educational science activities / Alex Kuskowski ; consulting editor, Diane Craig, M.A./reading specialist.
    pages cm. -- (Amazing super simple inventions)
  Audience: K to grade 4
  ISBN 978-1-62403-733-7
  1. Bell, Alexander Graham, 1847-1922--Juvenile literature. 2. Telephone--Experiments--Juvenile literature. 3. Telephone--History--Juvenile literature.
  4. Inventions--Juvenile literature. I. Title.
  TK6165.K87 2016
  621.385--dc23
                    2014049934

Super SandCastle™ books are created by a team of professional educators, reading specialists, and content developers around five essential components—phonemic awareness, phonics, vocabulary, text comprehension, and fluency—to assist young readers as they develop reading skills and strategies and increase their general knowledge. All books are written, reviewed, and leveled for guided reading and early reading intervention programs for use in shared, guided, and independent reading and writing activities to support a balanced approach to literacy instruction.

To Adult Helpers

The projects in this title are fun and simple. There are just a few things to remember to keep kids safe. Some projects require the use of wire and batteries. Also, kids may be using messy materials such as water. Make sure they protect their clothes and work surfaces. Review the projects before starting, and be ready to assist when necessary.

CONTENTS

TELEPHONES

AN INTRODUCTION

Today you can talk to a friend or family member anytime. Telephones make it possible.

The telephone is a machine. It lets people talk to each other from far away. They can be across the street or across the country!

A phone changes sound into data. The data is sent to another phone. It turns the data back into sound.

PARTS OF A TELEPHONE

receiver
(earpiece)

transmitter
(mouthpiece)

keypad

1	2	3
4	5	6
7	8	9
*	0	#

body

handset cord

TELEPHONE IS MADE FROM TWO GREEK WORDS!
tele = distance   phone = voice

Learn how the telephone works. Do experiments.
Discover the invention of the telephone for yourself!

ALEXANDER BELL

Alexander Graham Bell was a scientist, engineer, and inventor.

His most famous invention was the telephone. He experimented with sound as a kid. He built machines. One could speak words. He also trained his dog to bark words.

Bell's family inspired him. His mother and wife were **deaf**. He wanted to help them. He studied the human voice.

OTHER IMPORTANT PEOPLE

THOMAS WATSON

He helped Bell. He heard the first words on the telephone.

ROBERT HOOKE

He created a string telephone. Sounds made the string **vibrate**.

ELISHA GRAY

He invented an early telephone.

THEN TO NOW

A TIMELINE OF THE TELEPHONE

String telephones were invented. The string carried sound between two cans.

Bell invented the photophone. It was a phone that used light to carry sound.

Bell **introduced** the first candlestick telephone.

1667 **1876** **1880** **1892** **1915**

Alexander Graham Bell got a patent for his telephone. It was the first machine to carry voices over wire.

Bell and Watson made the first coast-to-coast call. The line stretched from New York to California.

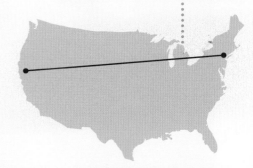

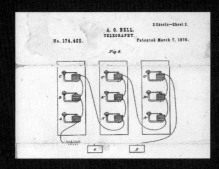

This is Alexander Graham Bell's telephone patent. A patent is a document. It says who owns an invention. Bell was the first to patent the telephone.

The first 9-1-1 call was made in Alabama.

EMERGENCY CALL 911

The first cell phone call was made.

1968   **1973**   **1984**   **2000s**

People started using caller ID. They knew who was calling before answering the phone.

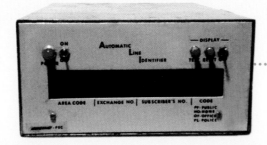

Smartphones became popular. They are small computers. People can use them to go online and get e-mail.

BE AN INVENTOR

Learn how to think like an inventor!

Inventors have a special way of working. It is a series of steps called the Scientific Method. Follow the steps to work like an inventor.

THE SCIENTIFIC METHOD

1. QUESTION

What question are you trying to answer? Write down the question.

2. GUESS

Try to guess the answer to your question. Write down your guess.

3. EXPERIMENT

Think of a way to find the answer. Write down the steps.

KEEP TRACK

There's another way to be just like an inventor. Inventors make notes about everything they do. So get a notebook. When you do an experiment, write down what happens in each step. It's super simple!

4. MATERIALS

What supplies will you need? Make a list.

5. ANALYSIS

Do the experiment. What happened? Write down the results.

6. CONCLUSION

Was your guess correct? Why or why not?

MATERIALS

6-volt lantern
battery

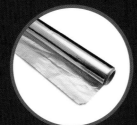

aluminum foil

cell phones

chair

flashlight

freezer bag

headphones

large dowel

large pot

metal measuring
cup

metal measuring
spoon

metal tin

Here are some of the materials that you will need.

painter's tape

plastic cup

pliers

rubber bands

ruler

scissors

Slinky

string

tuning fork

uncoated
copper wire

vinegar

water bottle

METAL MUSIC

Make sounds that will be music to your ears!

MATERIALS: string, ruler, scissors, metal measuring spoon, pen, plastic cup

Vibrations cause sound. The **vibrations** move through the air. They are called sound waves.

HOW DOES IT WORK?

The metal vibrates when the pen taps it. The vibrations create sound waves. The string carries the waves to the cup. The bottom of the cup vibrates. This makes the sound you hear.

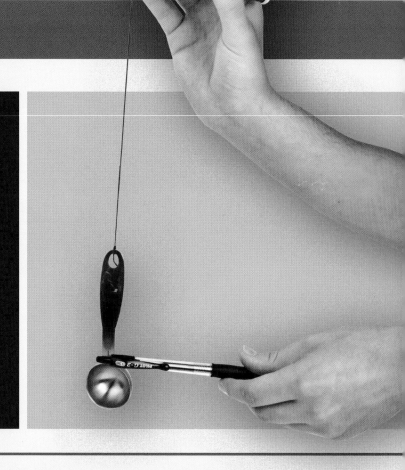

MAKE METAL MUSIC

① Cut a piece of string 12 inches (30 cm) long.

② Tie one end of the string to the measuring spoon.

③ Use the pen to poke a small hole in the bottom of the cup.

④ Thread the other end of the string through the hole.

⑤ Tie a few knots in the string on the inside of the cup. Make it so that the string doesn't slip through the hole.

⑥ Hold the cup to your ear. Tap the spoon with the pen.

STRING PHONE

Step back in time with the original telephone!

MATERIALS: string, ruler, scissors, pen, 2 plastic cups

The very first telephone was a string telephone. It did not use electricity.

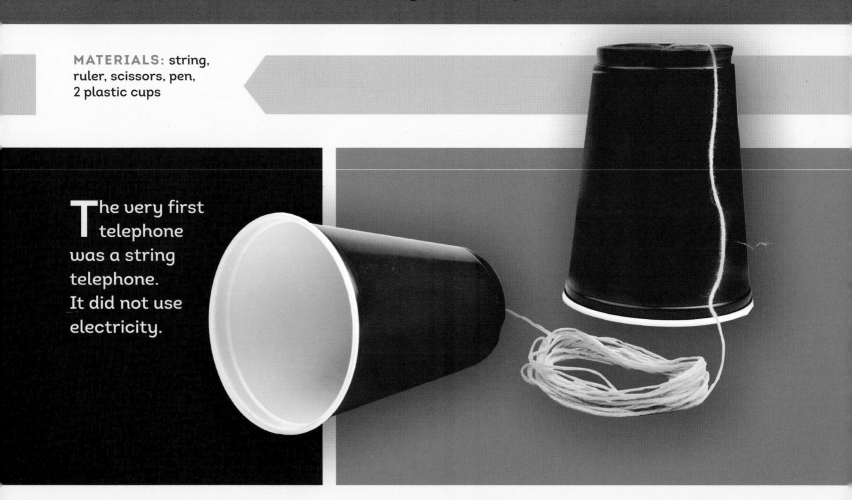

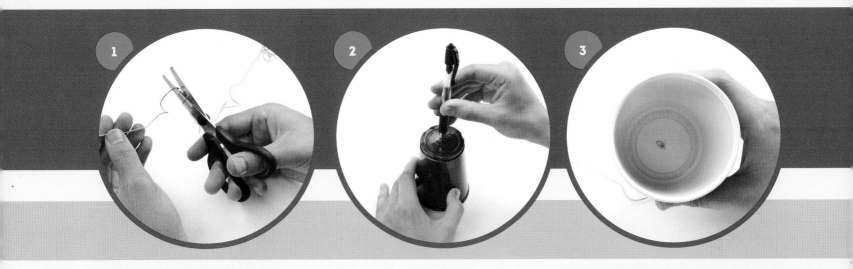

MAKE A STRING PHONE

1 Cut a piece of string 25 feet (7.6 m) long.

2 Use the pen to poke a small hole in the bottom of each cup.

3 Thread each end of the string through the hole in a cup. Tie a few knots in the string on the inside of the cups.

4 Hand one cup to a friend. Walk slowly away from each other until the string is tight.

5 Have your friend hold the cup over his or her ear. Whisper into your cup. Can your friend hear you?

HOW DOES IT WORK?

Your voice makes the bottom of the cup **vibrate**. The vibrations move along the string. They make the bottom of your friend's cup vibrate. Your friend can hear the sound.

CHAT ROOM

Make a line only you and your friends can use!

Old telephones used shared lines. You could hear your neighbors talking when you picked up your phone.

HOW DOES IT WORK?

The sound waves move the strings whenever anyone speaks. All the strings move. Everyone can hear the same thing through his or her cup.

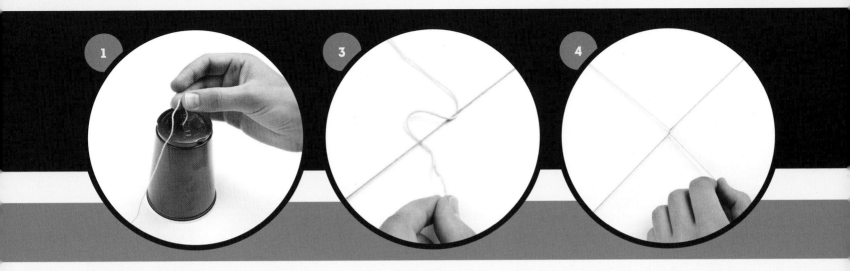

MAKE A CHAT ROOM

1. Make two string telephones following the directions on page 17.

2. Have two friends hold the cups of one telephone.

3. Wrap the telephone strings together.

4. Make sure the strings are straight.

5. You and a third friend hold the cups of the second telephone.

6. Take turns talking and listening.

SOUND WAVES

Make your own waves!

MATERIALS: large dowel, Slinky, painter's tape, 2 chairs

Sound waves move through the air. They carry **vibrations**. See how they move.

HOW DOES IT WORK?

The Slinky moves like sound waves. Air moves when an object nearby vibrates. It carries the sounds as it moves in a wave.

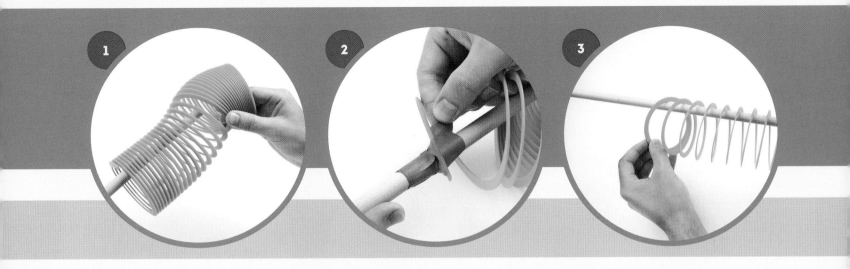

MAKE SOUND WAVES

1 Put the dowel through the Slinky.

2 Tape one end of the Slinky to the dowel.

3 Spread the Slinky out along the dowel. Stretch it lightly. Tape the other end to the dowel.

4 Rest the dowel ends across the backs of two chairs.

5 Pull gently on one end of the dowel. Watch the Slinky move. Pull on it harder. Then pull more gently again. How does the movement change?

TUNING FORK

Recreate Bell's idea to make a ring in your ears!

MATERIALS: copper wire, ruler, pliers, 6-volt lantern battery, metal measuring cup, headphones, tuning fork, vinegar

Bell built a machine like this. It helped him invent the telephone!

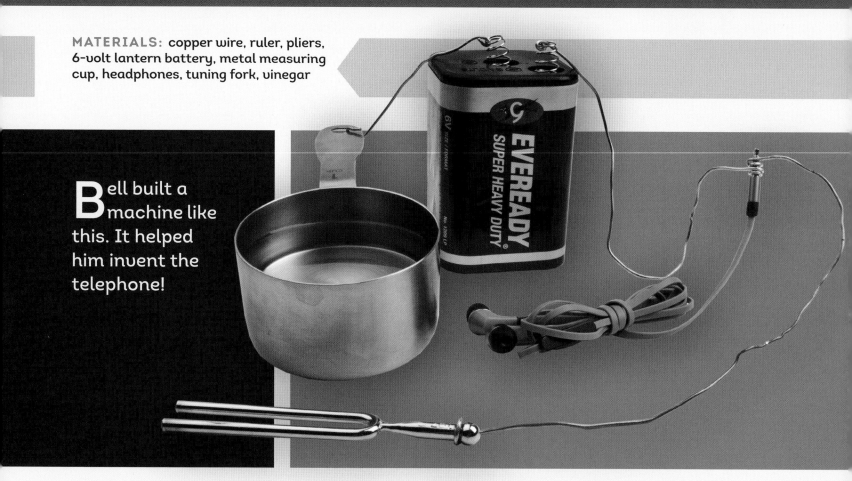

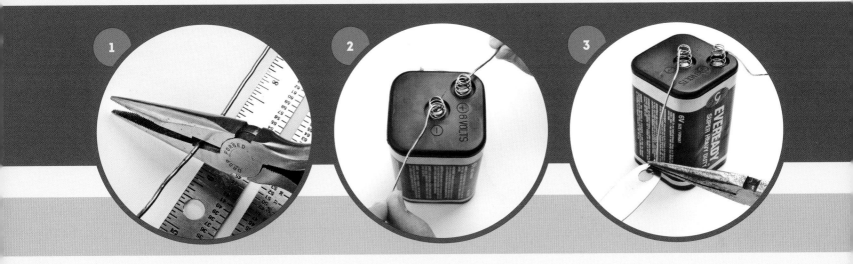

MAKE BELL'S TUNING FORK EXPERIMENT

1 Cut three pieces of wire. Make one 6 inches (15 cm) long. Make two of them 8 inches (20 cm) long.

2 Connect the short wire to the **negative terminal** on the **battery**. Wrap the end of the wire around the metal coil. Connect a long wire to the **positive terminal**.

3 **Attach** the measuring cup to the other end of the long wire.

continued on next page

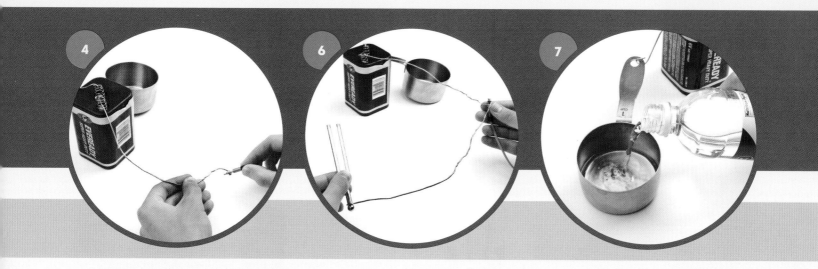

MAKE BELL'S TUNING FORK EXPERIMENT (CONTINUED)

④ Wrap the other end of the short wire around the headphone plug.

⑤ Wrap one end of the third wire around the headphone plug.

⑥ Wrap the other end around the tuning fork.

⑦ Fill the measuring cup with vinegar.

⑧ Put the headphones on. Hit the tuning fork **tines** on the edge of the table. Quickly lower the tines into the vinegar. Make sure the tines enter the vinegar at the same time. What do you hear?

9 Hit the **tines** again. This time, lower the tuning fork sideways. One tine should enter the vinegar before the other. Does it sound different?

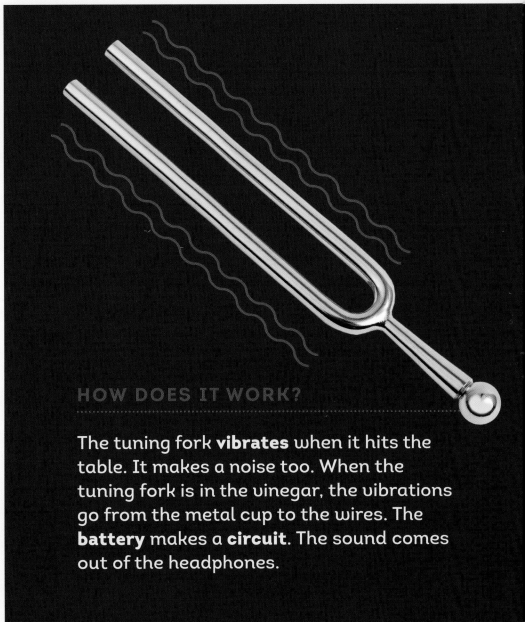

HOW DOES IT WORK?

The tuning fork **vibrates** when it hits the table. It makes a noise too. When the tuning fork is in the vinegar, the vibrations go from the metal cup to the wires. The **battery** makes a **circuit**. The sound comes out of the headphones.

TRANSMIT LIGHT

Light can carry a message!

MATERIALS: water bottle, scissors, aluminum foil, rubber band, flashlight

Before Bell created the telephone, he made the photophone. The photophone used light to carry messages.

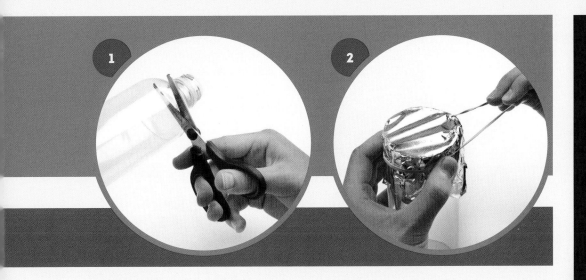

MAKE A LIGHT TRANSMITTER

① Cut off both ends of the water bottle.

② Cover one end with aluminum foil. Hold it in place with a rubber band.

③ Turn off the lights. Point the aluminum foil end toward a wall. Shine a flashlight at the aluminum foil. Speak into the open end of the bottle.

HOW DOES IT WORK?

Your voice made sound waves. The sound waves caused the foil to move. The foil moving changed the light on the wall.

Alexander Bell invented a way to capture that light. He changed it to sound.

FARADAY BOX

Make a cell phone jammer!

MATERIALS: 2 cell phones, freezer bag, metal tin with lid, large pot, aluminum foil

Cell phones use radio waves. Blocking the waves is easy. It's not magic. It's science!

MAKE A FARADAY BOX

1. Put one phone in a freezer bag. Zip the bag closed.

2. Put the phone in a metal tin. Put the lid on the tin.

3. Put the tin in the pot.

4. Cover the pot with aluminum foil.

5. Use the second phone to call the phone in the pot.

HOW DOES IT WORK?

The phone is inside two metal **containers**. The metal stops the radio waves from getting through. The phone inside will not ring.

CONCLUSION

Phones are part of daily life. They are everywhere, but they have changed a lot. This book is the first step in discovering what's behind your touch screen. There is a lot more to find out.

Learn more about telephone **technology**. Look online or at the library. Think of phone experiments you can do on your own.

Put on your scientist thinking cap and go on a learning journey!

QUIZ

1. What does the word telephone mean in Greek?

2. Alexander Graham Bell's mother and wife were **deaf**. TRUE OR FALSE?

3. Sound is caused by **vibrations**. What are the vibrations called when they travel through the air?

THINK ABOUT IT!

If you could call anyone in the world, who would you call?
What would you talk about?

Answers: 1. Distance voice 2. True 3. Sound waves

GLOSSARY

attach – to join or connect.

battery – a small container filled with chemicals that makes electrical power.

circuit – a system of elements that conduct electricity.

container – something that other things can be put into.

deaf – unable to hear.

introduce – to present or announce something new.

material – something needed to make or build something else.

negative terminal – the connector on a battery that energy flows into when used in a circuit.

positive terminal – the connector on a battery that energy flows out of when used in a circuit.

technology – the science of how something works.

tine – one of the points of a fork.

vibrate – to make very small, quick movements back and forth. The movements are called vibrations.